I LOVE IT WHEN YOU

_____

_____

_____

_____

OUR FAVORITE THING TO DO IS

_____

_____

_____

_____

YOU SMILE WHENEVER I

_____

_____

_____

_____

GRANDMA

I WROTE THIS BOOK ABOUT

YOU

THIS BOOK WAS WRITTEN BY

_____

_____

_____

IT WAS SO MUCH FUN WHEN WE

_____

_____

_____

_____

YOU ALWAYS HELP ME

_____

_____

_____

_____

I LOVE IT WHEN YOU TELL ME

_____

_____

_____

_____

YOU ARE REALLY HAPPY WHEN

_____

_____

_____

_____

I LOVE IT WHEN WE

_____

_____

_____

_____

THE FUNNIEST THING THAT YOU DO IS

_____

_____

_____

_____

YOU WILL ALWAYS BE THE BEST

_____

_____

_____

_____

I LOVE IT WHEN YOU CALL ME

_____

_____

_____

_____

YOU HAVE TAUGHT ME HOW TO

_____

_____

_____

_____

I AM PROUD THAT YOU ARE

_____

_____

_____

_____

YOUR FAVORITE FOOD IS

_____

_____

_____

_____

IT IS SO GOOD THAT YOU ALWAYS

_____

_____

_____

_____

OUR FAVORITE GAME TO PLAY IS

_____

_____

_____

_____

I LOVED IT WHEN WE WENT TO

_____

_____

_____

_____

THANK YOU SO MUCH FOR

_____

_____

_____

_____

ONE DAY I WOULD LOVE TO BUY YOU

_____

_____

_____

_____

SOMETIMES YOU MAKE FUNNY

_____

_____

_____

_____

I WISH WE HAD MORE TIME TO

_____

_____

_____

_____

I THINK YOU ARE SO COOL BECAUSE

_____

_____

_____

_____

YOU ARE THE KIND OF PERSON WHO

_____

_____

_____

_____

THE BEST THING ABOUT YOU IS

_____

_____

_____

_____

YOU ALWAYS SMILE EVEN WHEN

_____

_____

_____

_____

YOU ARE REALLY GOOD AT

_____

_____

_____

_____

I KNOW YOU LOVE ME BECAUSE YOU

_____

_____

_____

_____

YOU ARE
SO SMART
BECAUSE YOU

_____

_____

_____

_____

I LOVE HOW YOU ALWAYS

_____

_____

_____

_____

YOU
LOVE IT
WHEN I

_____

_____

_____

_____

IT WAS SO COOL WHEN YOU GAVE ME

_____

_____

_____

_____

I CAN'T WAIT UNTIL WE

_____

_____

_____

_____

WHEN I THINK OF YOU I ALWAYS

_____

_____

_____

_____

GRANDMA
I LOVE YOU
MORE THAN

_____

_____

_____

_____

MY FRIENDS THINK THAT YOU ARE

_____

_____

_____

_____

YOU ARE SUCH A GOOD

_____

_____

_____

_____

I LOVED IT WHEN YOU MADE

_____

_____

_____

_____

YOU INSPIRE ME TO

_____

_____

_____

_____

YOUR FAVORITE TV SHOW IS

_____

_____

_____

_____

YOU LOVE ME BECAUSE

_____

_____

_____

_____

YOU ALWAYS MAKE ME LAUGH WHEN

_____

_____

_____

_____

WHEN PEOPLE MEET YOU THEY THINK

_____

_____

_____

_____

YOU SHOULD WIN FIRST PRIZE FOR

_____

_____

_____

_____

YOU WERE PROUD OF ME WHEN I

_____

_____

_____

_____

I LOVE HEARING YOUR STORIES FROM

_____

_____

_____

_____

YOU ARE SO SPECIAL TO ME BECAUSE

_____

_____

_____

_____

I LOVE IT
WHEN YOU
COOK

_____

_____

_____

_____

THANK YOU
FOR FIXING
MY

_____

_____

_____

_____

YOU MAKE ME FEEL SPECIAL WHEN

_____

_____

_____

_____

YOUR FAVORITE SAYING IS

_____

_____

_____

_____

IT'S GREAT FUN WHEN WE

_____

_____

_____

_____

GRANDMA, I REALLY LOVE YOU BECAUSE

_____

_____

_____

_____

Made in the USA
Monee, IL
10 May 2023

33434821R10061